Learning About Landforms

Valleys

Ellen Labrecque

Raintree is an imprint of Capstone Global Library Limited, a company incorporated in England and Wales having its registered office at 7 Pilgrim Street, London, EC4V 6LB – Registered company number: 6695582

www.raintreepublishers.co.uk
myorders@raintreepublishers.co.uk

Edited by Rebecca Rissman, Daniel Nunn and Catherine Veitch
Designed by Steve Mead
Picture research by Elizabeth Alexander
Production by Victoria Fitzgerald
Originated by Capstone Global Library
Printed and bound in China

ISBN 978 1 4062 7225 3
17 16 15 14 13
10 9 8 7 6 5 4 3 2 1

British Library Cataloguing in Publication Data
A full catalogue record for this book is available from the British Library.

Acknowledgements
We would like to thank the following for permission to reproduce photographs: Corbis p. 22 (© NASA); Getty Images pp. 5 (Luis Davilla/Photodisc), 6 (Joe Cornish/Stone), 7 (Detlev van Ravenswaay /Picture Press), 10 submarine valley (David Doubilet/National Geographic), 11 rift valley (Nigel Pavitt), 14 (Shubert Ciencia/Flickr), 15 (Nigel Pavitt/AWL Images), 16 (National Geographic Creative/ Aaron Huey), 18 (David C Poole/Robert Harding World Imagery), 20 (Peter Adams/The Image Bank), 24 (David Madison/Lifesize), 25 (PREAU Louis-Marie/hemis.fr), 28 (Carol Rukliss/Flickr), 29 (J J D/ Photonica); naturepl.com pp. 8 (© Angelo Gandolfi), 13 (© Gavin Maxwell), 17 (© Anup Shah), 27 (© Daniel Heuclin); Science Photo Library p. 23 (© NOAA); Shutterstock pp. 4 (© Loskutnikov), 9 (© by Paul), 10 glacier valley (© bierchen), 10 river valley (© David Hughes), 11 canyon valley (© Josemaria Toscano), 11 gorge valley (© Karine Lazarus), 12 (© Francesco R. Iacomino), 19 (© deckard_73), 21 (© Lukas Hudec), 26 (© visceralimage).

Cover photograph of a valley in the Altai Mountains reproduced with permission of Shutterstock (© Pichugin Dmitry).

Every effort has been made to contact copyright holders of material reproduced in this book. Any omissions will be rectified in subsequent printings if notice is given to the publisher.

Contents

Some words are shown in bold, **like this.** You can find out what they mean by looking in the glossary.

What are landforms?

Look around when you are outside. You may see hills, valleys or caves. Earth is full of these natural landforms. This book is about valleys.

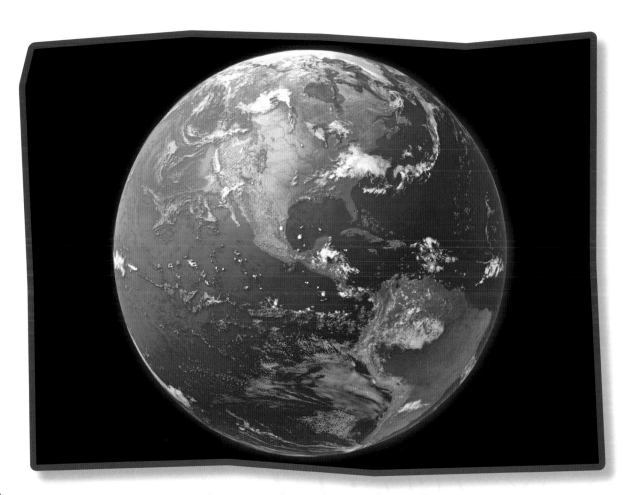

Earth is always changing. Earth's landforms are made in different ways over millions of years. Valleys are made when **erosion** wears down the land.

What are valleys?

A valley is a low area of land between mountains or hills. Mountains and valleys are always side by side. Some valleys are wide and flat. Others are deep, with steep sides.

The Valles Marineris is a huge valley on Mars.

Valleys can be found on land, under the ocean, and even on other planets! The deepest and longest valley in our **solar system** is on Mars.

How are valleys formed?

Valleys are made in two shapes: U-shaped valleys and V-shaped valleys. Flowing rivers and streams make V-shaped valleys. The water carves steep-walled sides and a narrow floor. These valleys look like the letter "V".

Glaciers, or big pieces of floating ice, make U-shaped valleys. The blocks of snow and ice move down mountains and carve away at the rock valley floor and sides. They create a "U" shape.

Different types of valleys

Valleys have all kinds of **climates**. They can be dry and dusty, icy and cold, or green and **fertile**. They also have a wide range of plant and animal life.

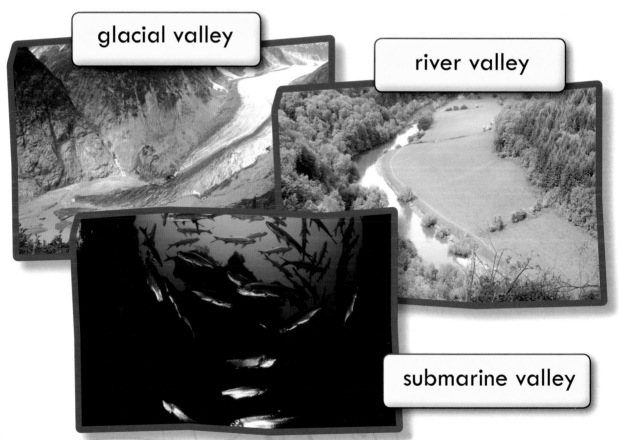

glacial valley

river valley

submarine valley

The six main kinds of valleys are glacial valleys, river valleys, submarine valleys, canyon valleys, gorge valleys and **rift** valleys.

canyon valley

gorge valley

rift valley

Canyons

Canyons are narrow valleys with steep sides and a river flowing at the bottom. Rivers are powerful. They wind back and forth, carve out banks and sculpt the walls.

During heavy rain, water breaks off rocks and stone. They fall from the steep sides and the canyon grows wider at the top than at the bottom.

Gorges

A gorge is a narrow valley with steep, rocky walls. They are smaller than canyons. But both have a river or stream flowing at the bottom. Gorges are made by rivers, streams or **glaciers**.

Gorges show layers of rock that go back millions of years. Scientists find **fossils** and ancient tools in gorges. These discoveries help explain how early humans lived.

Rift valleys

The surface of Earth is made up of huge rocks.
These parts of Earth are always moving.
Rift valleys are created when these rocks pull
apart. Rift valleys have steep, flat sides.

Baikal Rift Valley, Siberia

The Great Rift Valley in East Africa is still growing bigger. Scientists think in millions of years, it will split parts of East Africa from the rest of the **continent.** It will form a new island.

Glacial valleys

During the **ice age** long ago, ice covered large areas of Earth. The weight of the ice made it move like a slow river. Huge lumps of ice called **glaciers** moved slowly across Earth. They carved out deep valleys in the land.

U-shaped valley

Porsmork Valley in Iceland is a glacial valley.

Glaciers near the coldest places on Earth still create glacial valleys today.

River valleys

Rivers and streams make most of the valleys on Earth. As they flow down mountains, they carve out **channels** in the rock as the water finds a path to the sea.

Nile River Valley, Africa

Draa River Valley, Africa

If the river carves a gentle path to the sea, it will make a wide valley. If it has a steeper path, the valley will have sharp sides and a narrow channel.

Submarine valleys

Submarine valleys are under the ocean. They are the deepest parts of the ocean. Some of these valleys were made during the **ice age** long ago.

Mariana Trench is a submarine valley.

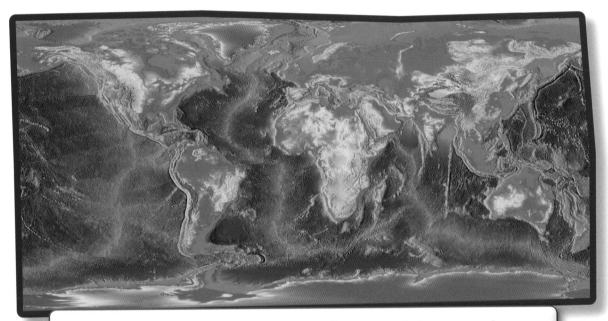

The dark blue areas on this world map show the submarine valleys in the world.

The surface of Earth is made up of huge rocks. These parts of Earth are always moving. Submarine valleys are created when these rocks pull apart.

Valley people

Many people all over the world live in valleys. The valleys that people live in are usually wide. Valleys have **fertile** lands that are good for growing **crops**. Valleys usually have fresh water flowing nearby.

The Loire Valley in France is one of the most fertile areas in all of Europe. It is called the "Garden of France" because so many fruit and vegetables grow in the valley.

Plants and animals

Many plants and animals live in valleys. Mountain lions, deer and smaller animals can be found in some valleys. Many **crops** are grown in valleys, too.

mountain lion

These pupfish live in Death Valley. They swim in water that can be as hot as 44 degrees Celsius!

Death Valley in California, United States is one of the driest and hottest places on Earth. Even so, many creatures live there.

Valleys today

Landforms are always changing. Water, ice and wind change valleys every day. The rocks that make up Earth are also always moving and changing the way valleys look.

glacier

Valleys are also in danger because of **global warming.** As the **climate** gets warmer, it melts the icy **glaciers.** The water flows down the mountains and changes the land below.

Glossary

channel length of water that connects two larger areas of water

climate weather conditions in a certain area

continent one of the large areas that Earth's land is divided into

crop plants that are grown for food

erosion process of the earth being worn away by water, waves, wind or glaciers

fertile capable of producing plants and vegetation

fossils remains of animal life found in rock

glacier slow-moving block of ice

global warming gradual increase of Earth's temperature

ice age period of time when large sheets of ice covered large areas of land

rift crack or split in something

solar system the Sun and the planets, including Earth, that move around it

Find out more

Books to read

Geography Wise: Rivers, Leon Gray
    (Wayland, 2012)

Investigate Geography: Landforms, Jane Penrose
    (Heinemann Library, 2010)

Landform Adventures: Canyon Hunters,
    Anita Ganeri (Raintree Publishers, 2012)

Websites to visit

www.nps.gov/deva/forkids/index.htm
Visit this site to learn more about Death Valley
in California.

www.worldatlas.com
Explore maps and landforms on this site.

Index